THE
MODERN
WITCH'S GUIDE
TO HAPPINESS

THE
MODERN
WITCH'S GUIDE
TO HAPPINESS

SELF-CARE RITUALS, MYSTIC GUIDANCE
AND MAGIC SPELLS
TO HARNESS YOUR POWER

LUNA BAILEY

Get Creative 6

Published in North America in 2021 by Get Creative 6, an imprint of Mixed Media Resources
104 West 27th Street, Third Floor, New York, NY 10001
www.sixthandspring.com

First published in Great Britain in 2019 by
Michael O'Mara Books Limited
9 Lion Yard
Tremadoc Road
London SW4 7NQ

Text and layout copyright © Michael O'Mara Books Limited 2019
Designed and typeset by Claire Cater
Art direction by Ana Bjezancevic
Photography by Roger Dixon
Cover design by Joe Vior

Additional illustrations from shutterstock.com (cover and pp. 20, 22, 24, 26–30, 32, 54, 59–61, 66–69, 71, 73 (bottom), 74–75, 85, 88, 93, 96, 100, 102, 108–109, 118)

Library of Congress Cataloging-in-Publication Data

Names: Bailey, Luna, author.
Title: The modern witch's guide to happiness : self-care rituals, mystic
    guidance and magic spells to harness your power / Luna Bailey.
Description: First edition. | New York, New York : Get Creative 6, 2021. |
    Includes index.
Identifiers: LCCN 2019056951 | ISBN 9781640210714
Subjects: LCSH: Witchcraft. | Happiness--Miscellanea.
Classification: LCC BF1566 .B248 2020 | DDC 133.4/3--dc23
LC record available at https://lccn.loc.gov/2019056951

2 4 6 8 10 9 7 5 3

Printed in China

Contents

Introduction

'It is time. You are ready. You have all the ability you need to see beauty in humble places, find happiness in unexpected things and summon strength from deep within. That is your power. That is your Magic.'

Being a witch is about healing, having faith, listening to our surroundings and intuitions. In essence, it speaks of our powers for love, strength and wisdom. Every day is a journey of discovery; we learn how to see with clarity, feel with our senses and connect with ourselves; and understand that, as witches, there is no limit to how alive we can feel. There are no dark or negative connotations to the word anymore. We have reclaimed it. We celebrate it as passionate, powerful and full of knowledge. Welcome, witch!

YOUR OWN PERSONAL MAGIC

'Witches listen to the secrets of the Earth, work in harmony with the powers of the moon and understand the longings of the human soul.'

DACHA AVELIN

Magic is a power that comes from within us all. It is up to us to develop, respect and use it for the good of ourselves and others. We have to honor this inner power, this deep-seated energy. By doing so, we can take ourselves on a journey of self-care, discovery and happiness.

This guide will help you dispel negativity and toxic energy from your life by examining the different ways you can give your inner witch a voice. There is not one single answer, not one golden rule and certainly not a right or wrong way to be a witch. It is something each of us must discover for ourselves.

My advice and teachings come with one disclaimer: that by opening ourselves up to different avenues of modern-day witchery – be they Tarot cards, crystals, spells or affirmations of self-care and self-worth – we can focus our minds on one single direction and destination: happiness. Of course, there are many definitions of happiness, and you will have your own. For me, a large part of it is about fulfillment. Connecting with the Magic that resides within us and surrounds us offers me that happiness, that fulfillment, in a truly unique and powerful way.

My guide will help you:

Focus on the ways we can harness our cosmic energy by exploring the teachings and guidance of astrology

Direct your psychic power into Tarot readings: how to get the best from the cards, how to reset your life with Tarot, and how to use spreads for different purposes

Connect with your body through self-care rituals and empower your mind

Embrace the Magical and healing power of nature, connect with the seasons and gain strength from the weather

Find and hone your intuition, strengthen your instincts and develop your senses

Summon your inner goddess by soaking yourself with belief in your energy

Trust in the powers working with you and strengthen the powers inside you

You picked up this book for a reason. Just as you are drawn to certain people and certain places, you are drawn to certain objects (like this book) by the energy they give. Let's start with that...

It Starts with a Breath

Stand still with both feet flat on the ground, and close your eyes.

Inhale. Exhale.

Did the simplicity of such an instruction take you by surprise?

Did you shut out everything around you, just for a nanosecond, and follow the command of living?

We can take the most simple power for granted, but what power it is – to focus our minds so completely on our bodies. On our chests rising and falling, of feeling the air entering our lungs and then being released again.

We take it for granted, perhaps, because in this modern world we forget the essence of ourselves. We forget the deep-seated energy that resides in each and every living thing: a rock, a blade of grass, us!

And combined with our brain power, it means that we are able to focus and direct this energy.

How lucky are those who have open minds and energy flowing freely. But we can all harness our power, and this guide will help you learn, adjust and focus.

So, let us take one more breath, and then we'll begin.

1

Getting Spiritual

'Each day has a new beginning, a new hope, a new blessing, so every day has something for us to be thankful for.'

I am often asked how a belief in Magic can help bring about positive changes in a person's life, and I reply that they have actually answered their own question ... Belief is the key! A trust in Magic is the recognition that our world is far more interesting and powerful than just what meets the eye. It's our fortune and privilege, as witches, to be able to see, feel and accept that influence.

It is our belief that we are not alone. We are in communication with and connected to everything around us. Therefore, we are able to ask for help when and where we need it. We open ourselves up to a world of possibility and wonder.

'Magic is simply you, being intentional about your life and working with all the beautiful energies around you.'

JESSICA DIMAS

INTENT AND MAGIC

Before you embark on any form of Magical ritual, spell or commitment, it is vital to have a clear intention. Any sort of ritual where you cleanse your thoughts and make your desires known can be considered a spell. But the more detailed, focused and organized your intent is, the more powerful the results will be.

I'm a firm believer that any person can tap into their own Magical reserve and bless their life – in fact, you are probably doing it all the time without realizing. Do you make a wish when you throw a coin into a fountain? Cross your fingers and hope for something in your head? These are all basic ways of conjuring Magic into your life, asking for help from an unknown force.

But casting an intent is stronger than wishes (which are often spontaneous, fleeting desires) as it is rooted in a 'will' – your will. The more focused, clear and organized your intentions are, the greater the chance of the universe listening and answering your spell.

Your intent is your purpose, your focus and your goal. Communication is the key, so it is critical to make this intent crystal clear. Making a statement before every ritual – sometimes called a 'statement of intent' – will give you a strong basis for any Magic you choose to perform. And it's vital that it's very specific. For example, 'I get the promotion at work I have been interviewed for and receive a pay raise of [fill in the amount you were aiming for].'

Three ways to show intent:

Verbalize it: Speak it clearly and loudly at the beginning of your spell. You can repeat this continually as a chant or just say it once. You can whisper it quietly or shout it from the rooftops.

Write it down: This can help focus your thoughts and phrasing of an intent. Be detailed in what your intention is by writing it on a piece of paper and folding it up afterwards.

Think it: Internalizing your intention and thinking your intention clearly before a ritual is just as powerful as the spoken word.

> 'Spells work by focusing your mind on your stated intention and action – summoning an energy from the universe in conjunction with your own.'

Energy

The universal energy that exists and is given out by the Earth and
all things on it (and around it) is there for us to channel and access
at all times. There is an infinite amount of energy and tapping
into it to help ourselves and others is the key to true Magic.

Every piece of matter gives out energy and we are all connected to it.
But as witches we are more aware of it, with ways to access and use it.

In its scientific form, think of electrons and particles
moving endlessly and tirelessly. All Magic begins with
harnessing that power with Magical intention.

POSITIVE AND POWERFUL: THE CHOICE OF WORDS

Using positive and strong words when casting your intent is imperative. If you are asking for help or guidance, you don't want to attract negative cosmic energy. Also, word your intent as a matter of 'fact' rather than 'I want'.

Likewise, when making your intent, don't use negative words like 'can't', 'won't', 'no' or 'not' as these bring negativity into your desires right away. For example, 'I don't want to be alone' is better phrased as, 'I have the power to attract the best people into my life.'

Intent vs. affirmation

Affirmations are usually one or two statements that retrain your mind into behaving in a certain way. For example, 'I will acknowledge my self-worth.'

Intentions are the actions you and the universal energies conspire to create. 'I get the promotion at work I deserve.'

What is your intent?

Whether you are communicating your intent with the universe or intuition, or higher power or deities, you are stating your desire and so you must be clear. What you are casting your intent for can be personal, or wider social outcomes.

Daily intentions

Setting intentions first thing in the morning is a great way to prime the energy for the day. To keep you focused, it can help to write them down, which you could do in a diary or on a piece of paper that you keep with you throughout the day. Or some people like to do it more publicly, on social media, and show the world their intention for the day:

'I intend to finish every task I set myself to do today.'

'I intend to accept whatever happens today as if I have chosen it.'

'I intend to channel delight into my day.'

Personal intentions

Love: You want to find a partner, or you have a relationship goal: 'I am with someone I connect with physically, emotionally and spiritually, and we are excited about our future together.'

Work: You want a promotion, pay raise or more recognition: 'I am recognized at work for doing what I love, my skills are in demand and I am paid well for doing my job.'

Social: You want to resolve an issue with a friend: 'I go on vacation with my best friend and we spend quality time with each other.'

Asking for help? Sometimes you want the universe to send its energy to a point outside your immediate circle:

△ You have relatives living abroad and you want to send them strength: 'I send love and positive energy to my brother as he fights his battle.'

△ You have a friend who is ill, and you want to send comforting, positive energy: 'The universe supports my purpose and I send love and the light of the universe to be with you.'

▽ You're an animal lover who wants to send protection to dogs who live on the streets: 'Cosmic energy, I command you to protect and shelter the dogs I cannot help myself.'

If you are asking for help or guidance from the universe, cosmic energy, spirit or higher power, be sure to send thanks in your final sentence. It is important to acknowledge the energy and power that has been brought to you, and to appreciate the Magical forces at work.

Getting Spiritual

There are a couple of other rules to consider when choosing your intent: you can't use your intent to harm others or to have a negative impact on other people or creatures; and you can't cast a spell that affects the free will of someone else. You must consider yourself in relation to the world around you and remember to find the purpose in your actions. Wishing someone harm isn't going to solve the problem of why they hurt you or why you want to punish them, so you have to focus instead on how you can overcome the situation, listening to your inner voice as moral guidance. A good healer friend of mine reminded me to always keep in mind the mantra: 'Do what you will, but harm none.'

Tip: Keep your intention focused and clear: 'I want to be in love' is too vague and too open. Do you know what kind of love you want? Do you want to fall in love with someone specific or are you searching for a particular kind of relationship? Do you want someone to fall in love with you? Do you want to learn to love yourself?

YOUR INTUITION

We talk about witches and healers as having a sixth sense, a guide that helps them see and feel without relying on their five other senses. This isn't simply a gift for the few – it can be felt in all of us if we open ourselves up to the idea of this non-physical perception. We can all master our third eye and our intrinsic power if we accept it, tune ourselves to it and learn to rely on it without question.

In fact, you're probably already aware of it, you just use another name. Our sixth sense, our intuition, the feeling in our guts, an inkling, a hunch ... call it what you will but this perception is key. Quite often we ignore this instinct and rely too heavily on our other senses, but in order to fully open up we need to see this as the most important awareness we possess.

It's time to harness the power of intention. This can be used
before you begin any spell as a way of focusing on your ritual.
You are saying to yourself and to the universal energies that
you are ready to begin. Light a candle as you repeat the words
aloud or stand outside barefoot as a way of grounding yourself.

A 'Call to Action' Spell

'Humbly, I call to thee, great cosmic energy.

Come to my side and be my guide.

I will keep my head up and my heart open.

Fill me with motivation.

Come to my side and be my guide,

I call to thee, cosmic energy.'

'The intuitive mind is a sacred gift and the rational mind
a faithful servant. We have created a society that honors
the servant and has forgotten the gift.'

ALBERT EINSTEIN

THE ART OF LISTENING

One of the key ways to develop your intuition is to go outside and embrace the
energies of nature. You are creating a connection to something bigger, Mother
Nature herself. Stand outside and simply listen; become attuned to the sounds,
the smells, the energy surrounding you. Stepping away from technology and other
distractions can awaken your basic survival intuition.

Other ways to develop your intuition:

Listen to your gut: The digestive system can give us physical indicators regarding a situation. This is often key to work success or failure. If your gut is telling you something is too good to be true – a business deal that will make you rich – there is probably a good reason.

Moment of insight: Do you sometimes get a flash of inspiration? Or suddenly get a thought about a person? Act on that insight right away if you can. A thought about a distant relative? It might be the cosmic energy at work and a relative is in need or distress. Why not give them a call and see?

Energy levels: Pay attention to how you feel when you are with certain people. Do they make you feel energized and happy, or do you feel drained when with them? There is a reason you are drawn to certain people and not to others. Listen to that instinct.

Focus on sleep: If you're struggling with a problem that you can't resolve, try giving your subconscious mind time to work out an answer. Before you go to sleep, ask yourself to come up with a solution while you sleep. This also works in the day if you take yourself to a peaceful place and ask yourself a question you've been struggling with. Take a few breaths and then listen to the answers. Try to ignore outside distractions or internal chatter and wait for a clear voice.

Listen to your dreams: In the same way you can get answers to problems as you sleep, focus on what your intuition might be telling you through your dreams. Dreams can often be symbolic and offer deeper messages than what appears on the surface.

Take time out: Try to give yourself a five-minute window of solitude and silence every day to escape into yourself. This might be taking time outside at a lunch break or going for a walk in the evening; you sometimes need these moments alone to engage and tune into your own intuition.

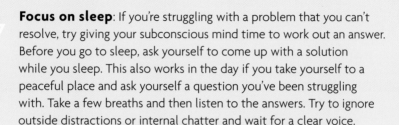

AWAKENING YOUR INTUITION

Wanting to accept Magic into your life is key to moving forward. Our spiritual awakenings can come at various stages of our lives, but there is no single reason why we become more open to the universe and our intuition. The awakening can happen for a number of reasons:

The birth of a child. A mother's intuition is an incredibly powerful tool, as is a father's, and one that comes to women after having a baby. Parents become tuned in to the needs of their child and quite often rely on their gut feelings more when it comes to their children.

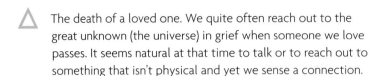

The death of a loved one. We quite often reach out to the great unknown (the universe) in grief when someone we love passes. It seems natural at that time to talk or to reach out to something that isn't physical and yet we sense a connection.

Sometimes having a massage, a Reiki session or any other form of healing can bring about a heightened 'sixth sense.' Your energy levels increase and you are more aware of protecting yourself from negative energy.

Experiencing a near-death situation. We have all heard stories of people who have not gone on a journey or decided not to take their normal route to work because of a gut feeling. This shift in perspective and actively reacting to it, such as making new arrangements, is a sign you have awoken to your intuition.

THE REWARDS

Using your intuition can have great benefits in your life. If you allow yourself to open up and listen to it, the rewards will be plentiful:

- You'll be more sensitive to the energies of the people and environments around you.

- You'll be able to tune into the feelings of others more easily.

- Your relationships will blossom as you appreciate and acknowledge those feelings.

- You'll feel more confident in decision making and your own judgment.

- You'll find yourself open to more ideas.

- Your creative side will develop as your imagination is awakened.

- You'll feel safer as you become more aware of trouble or danger around you.

Tip: Ultimately, your intuition is your connection to a higher wisdom. It's a trust and an energy emission; and energy never lies. Let that energy in, process it, express it and understand it. Know what feels right and trust that knowing.

2

Finding Your Rituals

'May the positive energy of the universe surround you and flow through you, bring love to your heart, peace to your mind and calm to your spirit.'

Ritual is at the heart of Magic, as it is through ritual that we achieve our Magical results. The ritual is the procedure or ceremony we perform in order to change something, usually in the physical world. Some may put the results down to coincidence, but this is to turn away from a source of great potential and power; the effects are very real, and Magical goals and the intent behind rituals should not be taken lightly. It doesn't matter how complex and long your ritual is or how simple and short, the successful practice of Magic is about belief. If you can believe your desired results will be accomplished, that itself is the ritual of Magic.

Self-care rituals can be used for lots of reasons, but for many of us, recognizing we need to take a little time for ourselves isn't always easy. Consider now, are you not letting go of things psychologically? Do you take on other people's problems as well as your own? Do you regularly become anxious about certain situations? These are all good reasons to prioritize self-care rituals. For me, and many other witches, self-care rituals are not just for when we need them but are a part of our daily lives.

The witch who is always ready to take on other people's problems and negative energies must be strong, full of positive energy and ready to embark on daily self-care rituals. The simple truth is that we cannot offer ourselves to the world if we aren't feeling balanced ourselves.

Ritual (noun) rit·u·al
Definition: A practice made sacred through mindful intention

Tip: With any healing or self-care rituals, it's important to listen to your body. If you are feeling tired or drained, allow your body time to release old, stagnant energy. Try going to bed super early for a few nights in a row, have a good cry, or, if you can, take a short nap! Whatever was suppressed will find its way out, and allowing your emotions to come through will help you to be more receptive to positive, assured energies.

THE SEVEN CHAKRAS

The seven chakras are important to mention now. The mainstream chakra system is based on the Hindu original that recognizes seven different 'wheels' or 'centers' of energy that allow energy to flow along the human body's spinal column. Modern-day witches understand that each one plays a significant role in maintaining a constant flow of energy connecting the whole body, mind, spirit and soul. Each chakra is a distinct energy center, representing a different emotional and physical state, so having one that is blocked can often lead to illness. The idea is to keep all the chakras (translation: 'wheels') open and in alignment with each other. Each chakra is associated with its own color as different colors possess different forms of energy. These follow the sequence in the colors of the rainbow.

THE CROWN CHAKRA	white or violet

Location: the top of the head

Linked to: the higher realms, universal healing, spirituality, beliefs

When in balance: you feel a sense of enlightened spiritual connection to others as well as higher realms; you feel like you are capable of anything and everything

If blocked: you feel alienated, confused, prone to prejudice; provokes a decline in overall excitement or motivation

Physical signs: sensitivity to light, headaches, problems with coordination, poor or inconsistent sleep habits

THIRD EYE CHAKRA	purple

Location: in the center of your brow

Linked to: intuition, imagination, visualization and clarity

When in balance: you trust your gut and plan according to your greatest goals

If blocked: you feel insignificant, that you don't understand people, you value rationality over intuition and have trouble making decisions

Physical signs: trouble sleeping, feeling clumsy, finding yourself unable to learn new things, headaches, earaches and eyesight issues

THROAT CHAKRA
blue or turquoise

Location: in the middle of your throat

Linked to: communication, self-expression, authenticity and creativity

When in balance: you are able to express yourself clearly and effectively; and have confidence in what you are saying

If blocked: you feel that you can't make yourself understood, you struggle to communicate effectively, can't find the right words or you don't think people want to hear what you have to say; you feel unable to say what you really want to say

Physical signs: sore throat, a tightening of the throat feeling, pain in the neck, thyroid problems, issues with breathing

HEART CHAKRA
green and pink

Location: directly above your heart

Linked to: compassion, love, acceptance, gratitude and meaningful relationships

When in balance: you feel emotionally open and able to offer empathy to others; you enjoy a deep sense of inner peace

If blocked: you feel restless and disgruntled, less compassionate, more impatient; you find it harder to trust people

Physical signs: anxiety, fatigue; you might struggle with a weakened immune system and high blood pressure

SOLAR PLEXUS CHAKRA
yellow

Location: at the top of your abdomen

Linked to: self-confidence and self-esteem, our actions

When in balance: you feel like you can accomplish anything

If blocked: you feel very low on self-esteem, insecure, unworthy, like a failure

Physical signs: indigestion, trouble with your memory; you might suffer from IBS (irritable bowel syndrome)

Finding Your Rituals

SACRAL CHAKRA   orange

Location: just below the belly button

Linked to: sexuality, desires, joy, sex drive, emotions and sensuality

When in balance: you are open to the world around you, very in tune with your desires and emotional needs

If blocked: you feel bored, resistant to change and uninspired; you might have a low sex drive and feel unpassionate

Physical signs: urinary problems, increased allergies, painful periods, lower back pain

ROOT CHAKRA   red or black

Location: the base of your spine

Linked to: your sense of stability, belonging, security and survival needs

When in balance: you feel calm and anchored in reality

If blocked: you feel anxious, panicked and uncertain; can manifest as paranoia and hypochondria

Physical signs: cold extremities, poor circulation, low energy levels/fatigue

Three simple ways to balance your chakras:

Learn yoga – certain poses help to balance the chakras.

Visualize each chakra being washed clean the
next time you are in the shower.

Surround yourself with the color of the chakra you want to balance
– colors possess energy that are complementary to particular chakras.

CHAKRA AFFIRMATIONS

There are lots of affirmations to help keep your chakras balanced and aligned. Below are a few of my favorites but feel free to use your own or research others. Only you will know what aspect of imbalance you need to concentrate on.

Crown: 'I am peaceful, calm and serene. I have everything that I need.'

Third eye: 'I am in the present and I can clearly see challenges before me.'

Throat: 'I can communicate clearly. I can say no when necessary. I express myself freely.'

Heart: 'I am open to healthy and nurturing relationships. I am loved, I am loving.'

Solar plexus: 'I am valuable and I am powerful. I can realize my dreams.'

Sacral: 'I am kind and compassionate. I naturally generate new ideas.'

Root: 'I am grounded and connected to the Earth.'

Mini Chakra Cleanse

Close your eyes and imagine your seven chakras as seven colored balls stacked one on top of the other. Visualize this colored stack of balls inside the center of your body and now imagine a beam of clear, pure white light going through the middle of the balls. Picture the white light cleansing each ball. Start at the base, your red root ball, and inspect it in your mind. If it is glowing with light, it is perfectly cleansed and you can move up to the next ball, your orange (sacral) ball. Repeat this inspection with each ball, checking the light is shining brightly from each one and they are all the same size. If one seems bigger, mentally adjust its size to match the others. You now have a bright, shining rainbow of cleansed chakras running through you.

SELF-CARE

'Self-care rituals' definition: The little things we do to nourish or sustain our mental and physical health and connect with our intuition.

Before we start dealing with self-care, we have to know how we feel at any given point and how we can change that energy within. Sometimes we forget that looking after ourselves is the key to moving forward, and being successful (whatever we envision our success looking like). That can only come about if we are in tune with our energies and know how to harness the more positive ones. The following ideas relate to general self-care and draw from the different chakra influences.

Top five easy self-care ideas

1. Wear color – simple really, because you are probably drawn to different colored clothes depending on your mood, so you should listen to what your wardrobe choice is telling you. We are attracted to color the way we are attracted to people and clothes – how they make us feel. The colors of the different chakras can help guide your choices here.

2. Spend time with friends and people who uplift and inspire you with positive energy. It's not rocket-science, is it? Joining a group, whether it's a local book club, pottery class, or a Reiki group on Facebook, can connect you with more of these excellent people.

3. Get your daily nature fix – this is a very important part of my self-care ritual. I take time out every morning to ground myself and connect with Mother Nature. A few moments of solitude and concentrating on my breathing is a key part of my daily routine.

4. Be honest – the more authentic and honest you are as a person, the more you will get back. Are you being true to yourself? Are you projecting a particular image on social media, for example? Don't be afraid to show the real you – you'll find people will respond to you in a more positive and energetic way.

5. Be of service to others – it's well understood that putting our energy into helping others brings us something in return. But the key is not to forget the reverse: as well as being someone offering to help, be the person who asks for help too.

Negative Energy: A Daily Cleanse

Ridding yourself of negative energy can become part of your daily self-care ritual (or a once-in-a-while spell if you prefer) as it is a short and focused affirmation. Light a white candle and set your intention to protect and clear your energy by saying aloud:

*'I dedicate this candle to the light and ask
for protection to surround me.'*

Your intention is to expel all the negative energy around you by commanding the negative energy to enter the flame and burn away.

RAVING ABOUT REIKI

Definition of Reiki (Japanese word):
Universal life energy. Pronounced ray-key.

The practice of Reiki is defined as: 'A healing technique based on the principle that the therapist can channel energy into the patient by means of touch, to activate the natural healing processes of the patient's body and restore physical and emotional well-being.'

Reiki is a Japanese technique developed over a hundred years ago and based on a simple principle that we are governed by an energy flow that controls our physical, mental and emotional well-being. As witches we understand the healing process of Reiki is an important aspect of self-care awareness, promoting positive and balanced energy flows throughout our bodies. Just as we know energy nourishes and nurtures every living thing, the energy channels in our bodies need to have an uninterrupted flow in order for us to function and achieve emotional balance. Similar to yoga and meditation, this wellness practice works together with the concept of chakras to allow the positive energy to flow through your body unhindered.

The Five Principles of Reiki

Just for today, I will not anger.

Just for today, I will not worry.

Just for today, I will be grateful for all my blessings.

Just for today, I will work with honesty and integrity.

Just for today, I will be kind to all living beings.

Benefits of Reiki:

△ Promotes personal awareness

△ Helps develop meditative states

△ Fosters natural self-healing

△ Balances energies in the body

△ Gives a sense of well-being and happiness

△ Heightens intuition

△ Reduces stress and anxiety

△ Strengthens self-esteem

△ Helps ease anger and mood swings

△ Improves sleep

△ Encourages mental clarity

Energy healing: Any therapy which stimulates and feeds the energy flow in or around the body to restore balance on all levels – mental, emotional, physical and spiritual.

Self-treatment tips

If you are a qualified Reiki healer, you know the benefits of daily self-healing, but this shouldn't be embarked on by those who are not trained. It takes a while to become a qualified healer, and the first thing you learn to do is heal yourself. You have to have the belief you can heal yourself – only then can you practice on friends and family.

That said, there are some lovely Reiki-style exercises and tips you can follow in a whole healing sense to help clear your chakras. For example, sit cross-legged on the floor or sit in a chair with both feet flat on the ground (grounded). With your back straight, focus on breathing in and out in a steady motion. Visualize the seven chakras aligned from the crown to the base of your spine. Now breathe in and visualize a white light coming in from your crown, down through all the chakras and out of your feet as you exhale. Repeat a few times as necessary to rebalance yourself.

FINDING SPACE FOR MAGIC

Magic spells, rituals and affirmations can all be carried out anywhere at anytime. But sometimes we need a place to focus ourselves and this can be done through an altar. Simply defined as a raised structure or place used for worship or casting spells, it is a place of concentration and calm for you.

Creating your altar

While an altar is certainly a personal site, when first creating one there are a few items considered ideal in making it a place for creativity, spiritual growth and guidance.

The following list might help you know where to begin but it is in no way exhaustive. Remember, every item placed on your altar should feel relevant to or resonate with you.

 An altar cloth: Colorful material designates the space further and can help color work evolve. But don't feel you have to choose just one color and never change it, or that it needs to be a specific color in order to be effective. Go with colors that you are drawn to, patterns that you find give off positive vibes. Mix and match different materials and textures. Have fun choosing!

 Salt: This is regarded as an important element to an altar. It is protective and purifying and represents the Earth's energy.

 The elements: Have an item for each element but don't feel you have to stay traditional or use tools that might not feel comfortable to you. The more personal the items you use, the more personal the energy of your altar.

 Earth: This can be a potted plant, a rock or a crystal that you are drawn to. Or what about a pine cone you've found on a walk?

 Fire: Candles are traditional, especially a white candle that is then used to light the other candles. But a battery powered candle is just as effective if you are worried about flames.

△ Air: Burning incense is a common representation of air but a feather is equally significant.

△ Water: Usually a chalice or a cup, but what about a beautiful seashell you found last summer and brought home? Or a small water fountain?

△ Spirit: This could be represented by a candle, pentacle or any image of a god or goddess that you feel drawn to.

△ A notebook or diary: If you are doing any written work with your ritual, keeping a notepad on the altar can help it absorb the energy.

Your altar should feel personal and creative to you, and you alone. Make it authentic to your personality, your goals and your needs. If you are setting up for a specific ritual or a spell, make sure you focus entirely on the purpose of the spell by adding to your basics with elements or items you want to charge or cleanse. For example, as a writer, if I want to charge a notepad to be full of creativity, ideas

and brilliance, I center the notepad on my altar, light the candles around it and sometimes place a crystal on top (citrine crystals are good). Either with a hand placed on it, or by simply looking at it, I charge it mentally with my positive energy until my intuition tells me it's full of good vibrations.

Tip:
Color Magic concerns placing items of different colors around your home to create different energies. It's commonly used with candles and spells – we use green candles for evoking money spells, for example.

DOs and DON'Ts when creating an altar

DO remember that an altar is personal to you and you shouldn't become fixated on a particular set of items that you are told are essentials (even the ones I've listed above shouldn't be regarded as essential). Add what feels right to you.

DON'T position your altar in a place that is constantly being used by others who might not understand its significance to you. For example, if your altar is on a table by the front door, it is in a place that people will pass frequently, and it might be prone to having things knocked over or being used for other things.

DON'T think you have to buy a specific piece of furniture for your altar. A windowsill, a bedside table, a wall shelf, a table ... the surface doesn't matter; the important thing is that it is in a place that won't be disturbed regularly.

DO cleanse the area where you are going to create your altar. Do this by burning sage or incense and saying your intentions for the space: 'With this sage I banish any negative energy from my space.'

DO fill your altar with items that are both functional to your Magical needs and symbolic and personal to you. It should be a point of peace and calm to you, filled with things you love.

DON'T think that you must have items arranged in perfect symmetry. Some people prefer a more organic approach to placement. Rearrange them as many times as you need to until you find a balance that feels right to you.

DO remember that each item should have a purpose, and put each item on your altar with intention. It should symbolize you and your unique energy.

DO remember when you are creating an altar that you are inviting particular energies to protect and guide whatever ritual, intention or celebration you are working with at that time. Therefore...

DON'T be nervous about changing your altar as your needs and intentions change.

Activate your altar!
Once you have set all the pieces in a balance
and placement that you are happy with,
bring the altar alive by lighting the candles
and burning the incense. Spend time giving
thanks for your spiritual workplace.

Bless This House Spell

Your home is your sacred place and a sanctuary for your energies. It is a place to protect as well as one to seek comfort from, and this short house blessing can be performed as many times as necessary – you might have just moved in, or had an unwelcome visitor, or you may just feel the need to ask the universe for extra protection in your dwelling.

During a full moon, burn sage and repeat the following aloud as you walk through your house:

'Bless this house
May peace dwell within
Protect all that enter
Whether friend or kin
Bless every door, window and wall
And cupboard and room and protect us all.
So mote it be.'

HEALING HERBS

Whether it's in a shop or out in the garden, I love selecting herbs that I feel most intuitively drawn to. I will then take them home and research their properties. All herbs can aid healing and self-care (although be aware that certain herbs can be poisonous so it's important to know what you've got). Each one can be made part of your Magical journey, depending on the purpose of your spell.

Ten Magical Herbs and Uses

| SAGE | cleansing * knowledge * healing * peace |

Tip: Burning sage will dispel negative energy and cleanse rooms and objects.

| ROSEMARY | memory * protection * cleansing |

Tip: Wear a stem around your neck when reading or studying to aid information retention.

| BASIL | confidence * money * health |

Tip: Use basil in your water when you next mop your floor to bring prosperity to your home.

| BAY LEAF | beauty * luck * purification |

Tip: Write a wish or desire on a bay leaf and then burn it, visualizing your desire as already being true.

| THYME | affection * clarity * courage |

Tip: Add a little thyme into your last meal of the day for restful, peaceful dreams.

| PENNYROYAL | money * strength * protection |

Tip: If you own your own business, try leaving a sprig by the front door of your shop or business to draw in customers and prosperity.

| **MINT** | energy * love * healing |

Tip: Place on your altar to draw in positive energy.

| **OREGANO** | comfort * strength * vitality |

Tip: Use oregano tea as a mouthwash to sooth toothache.

| **CHIVES** | love * warding * stimulation |

Tip: Hang a bouquet of chives by your front door to keep out unwanted visitors.

| **CHAMOMILE** | money * success* anti-stress |

Tip: Burn as an incense for calm meditation and sleep.

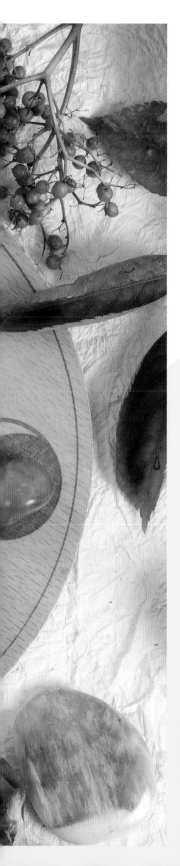

3

Harnessing Your
Cosmic Energy

'Astrology is a language.
If you understand this
language, the sky speaks
to you.' DANE RUDHYAR

Taurus? Aries? Leo? You are probably well aware of what zodiac sign
you are according to the date of your birth and the characteristics
associated with that sign. But astrology is far more fascinating and
complex than just that.

The study of astrology is as important and logical today as it was
hundreds of years ago, and its interpretation remains the same – the
positioning of the planets at any given time has an effect on our lives,
our personalities and the Magic we perform. We can study this ancient
science in its simplest form (reading your horoscope in a magazine) or we
can delve deeper into our astrological charts, and discover exactly how
the movement of each planet and star affects not just our very essence,
but how it shapes the behaviors and personalities of others too.

While most astrologers I know operate in a highly intuitive way, at its
heart astrology remains a study of people and their nature, based upon
the organized dance of the planets and stars.

The information about a person and their personality traits is linked to where the sun, moon and planets were at the time of their birth. Astrologers will take the date, place and exact time of your birth, and place it on a circular chart. That chart can be treated like a map to the self. OK so far?

It's probably worth saying at this point that there are hundreds if not thousands of books and websites dedicated to the study of astrology. I am only touching on the very basics here. So, if your interest has been piqued, you'll have lots of lovely cosmos-based material to study! Go find an astrologer, get a reading, join a group or take a course and you never know, you might find this Magical language a lifelong passion.

Tip: It's common to consult professional astrologers when planning big events; this is called electional astrology. It will help you find the most appropriate time for an occasion. A friend of mine used a professional astrologer to chart an ideal date and time for her wedding. After seeing the chart, the couple moved their afternoon wedding to an earlier lunchtime slot due to the astrologer's forecast of perfect conditions. Astrology helped her manifest a propitious start to her marriage.

ZODIAC SIGNS

Most of us think we know what zodiac sign we are because of our dates of birth but these are actually our sun signs and only one part of the astrology puzzle. So, making assumptions that a Leo and a Pisces shouldn't be romantically involved is oversimplifying the whole shebang. In order to deduce things such as compatibility, we would also need to know about our moon signs, as they can tell us far more about our emotional selves. And we also need to know our rising (ascending) signs, which reveal more about how we interact with the world.

In astrology, the sky is split into twelve sections of the zodiac, and as the Earth spins, the sun, moon and planets all move through those different zodiac sections. The closer to Earth a planet is, the faster it zips through all those sections or signs. For example, the moon works its way through all twelve sections in twenty-eight days, staying in each bit for about two days. The sun spends roughly thirty days in each sign, taking about a year to move through them all – this is why we have twelve signs for the twelve months of the year.

THE TWELVE HOUSES

Each of these twelve zodiac sections is called a house, and each house represents a different part of your life.

△ 1st house: personality, appearance, how you see yourself, your general outlook on life

△ 2nd house: your sense of worth, self-esteem, daily routines, how you spend money

▽ 3rd house: communication, siblings, childhood, intellect, early education

▽ 4th house: home (where you are living now and when you were born), family, upbringing, ancestry

△ 5th house: love, romance, children, entertainment, enjoyment, creativity

△ 6th house: health, exercise, daily routines, activities, fitness

▽ 7th house: marriage, separation, divorce, partners at work or in a personal relationship

▽ 8th house: death and rebirth, sex, material possessions, taboo subjects

△ 9th house: spirituality, learning, teaching, long-distance travel, inspiration, optimism

△ 10th house: career, fame, public image, reputation, ambition

▽ 11th house: friendships, society, hopes, aspirations, groups, clubs

▽ 12th house: mysteries, the unconscious, endings, old age, prison, hospitals, methods of confinement

Each house is ruled by a sign of the zodiac which gives it its energy. All of the signs have a positive and negative side. 'Healthy' people tend to exhibit the positive traits in the list below while 'unhealthy', distressed people may well display the negative traits. Each sign of the zodiac also has a symbol (called a glyph) and an associated planet. Note that witches and astrologers tend to talk about the sun and moon as planets as this is how they were regarded in ancient times, even if modern astronomers might roll their eyes.

1ST HOUSE	Zodiac sign: Aries ♈	Planet: Mars
Personality traits: adventurous, courageous, confident, assertive, aggressive, hot-tempered, competitive		
2ND HOUSE	Zodiac sign: Taurus ♉	Planet: Venus
Personality traits: loyal, patient, persistent, affectionate, romantic, grounded, stubborn, selfish		
3RD HOUSE	Zodiac sign: Gemini ♊	Planet: Mercury
Personality traits: intelligent, adaptable, curious, chatty, inconsistent, superficial		
4TH HOUSE	Zodiac sign: Cancer ♋	Planet: Moon
Personality traits: emotional, family focused, compassionate, cautious, prone to mood swings, dramatic		
5TH HOUSE	Zodiac sign: Leo ♌	Planet: Sun
Personality traits: enthusiastic, bold, courageous, creative, loving, arrogant, bossy		
6TH HOUSE	Zodiac sign: Virgo ♍	Planet: Mercury
Personality traits: practical, reliable, perfectionist, helpful, intelligent, critical, prone to worry, picky		

> 'Astrology is a life-giving elixir to mankind.'
>
> ALBERT EINSTEIN

7TH HOUSE	Zodiac sign: Libra ♎	Planet: Venus

Personality traits: impartial, diplomatic, romantic, idealistic, tactful, indecisive, dislikes confrontation

8TH HOUSE	Zodiac sign: Scorpio ♏	Planet: Pluto

Personality traits: passionate, sexual, loyal, intuitive, heroic, jealous, vengeful, unforgiving

9TH HOUSE	Zodiac sign: Sagittarius ♐	Planet: Jupiter

Personality traits: optimistic, funny, happy, honest, enthusiastic, generous, inspiring, fickle, jealous, blunt

10TH HOUSE	Zodiac sign: Capricorn ♑	Planet: Saturn

Personality traits: practical, determined, cautious, disciplined, diplomatic, selfish, proud

11TH HOUSE	Zodiac sign: Aquarius ♒	Planet: Uranus

Personality traits: innovative, honest, loyal, original, rebellious, inflexible, closed-minded

12TH HOUSE	Zodiac sign: Pisces ♓	Planet: Neptune

Personality traits: kind, sensitive, gentle, shy, unconfident, weak-willed, prone to depression

Astrology and Tarot

While astrology is all about calculations and plotting, Tarot is intuitive and conceptual. But like most opposites, they complement each other beautifully and combining them can provide a profound insight into your reading. Each of the major Arcana cards in Tarot corresponds with the moon, stars and planets within the zodiac, but, like most Magical practices, it's up to you what weight to assign to the astrology of the card within the context of a reading – if at all.

PLOT YOUR BIRTH CHART

If you want to plot your own birth chart, which is completely unique to you and provides a snapshot of the planetary coordinates at the exact time of your birth, the three most important aspects of the chart are your sun, moon and rising signs.

Your sun sign: the sign of the zodiac where the sun was when you were born

Your moon sign: the sign that the moon occupied at the time of your birth

Your rising sign (ascendant): the zodiac sign that was on the eastern horizon at the moment of your birth (hence the need for an exact time of birth)

So... let's piece this together bit by bit.

Your sun sign represents your essence – the true you and the basis of your personality.

Your moon sign represents your emotional self, how you respond to others and your intuitive instincts about other people.

Your ascending sign is how you present yourself to the world, how you appear to others, and their first impressions of you.

Go online, and you'll see hundreds of websites and online tools that can help you plot your birth chart. It really is that simple!

Tip: Some people have the same sun sign as their rising sign and this is sometimes called a 'what you see is what you get' type personality. Others might seem like a certain sign (the way they portray themselves to the world) but are actually born under a different sun sign.

The planets

The last factor in a full astrological chart is the different planets and what they represent. You have the sun, the moon and all the planets in your chart. Each represents a different aspect of who you are. Just as knowing where the sun is on your astrological chart (i.e. your sun sign) can reveal a lot about your true nature, so can knowing about each of the planets. The following is a list of planets and what parts of your life they reflect. On your astrological chart you'll be able to see how the location of each one works. So, if Venus is in the 3rd house, for example, the house of communication, you'll likely find you are naturally chatty and engaging, and can easily fall into conversation.

Sun: your true nature, your essence

Moon: your emotions, feelings, intuition, relationship with your mother and women in general

Mercury: your intellect, how you communicate, learn and evaluate information

Venus: love, how you interact in a relationship, romance, physical beauty

Mars: passion, energy, what makes you determined

Jupiter: luck, optimism, hope, how you see life

Saturn: restraint, challenge, safety and security

Uranus: inspiration, rebellion, creativity

Neptune: imagination, dreams, mystical experiences

Pluto: the way you handle power, upheaval, transformation

North node*: what you are aspiring to accomplish, characteristics you are trying to learn

South node*: what you have learned and perhaps overdone

* The north and south nodes of a birth chart are lunar nodes and useful astrological pointers that guide us towards our most fulfilling spiritual paths. The lunar nodes are directly opposite each other in the chart and aren't planets, but rather mathematical points on the chart that fall into two opposite zodiac signs. So, if your north node is in Capricorn, your south node will be in its opposite sign of Cancer.

SEVEN IS THE MAGIC NUMBER

Ever heard of planetary days? The seven days of the week correspond to the seven fixed planets of astrology and can help you plan your Magical endeavors. Depending on the area of change you want your Magic to work in, certain days offer stronger conditions than others due to their connection with certain planets. As a result, it's a good idea to time your Magic on the day of the planet under which it falls.

Day of the week	Planet	Focus of Magical action
Sunday	Sun	Beginnings, goals, achievements, success
Monday	Moon	Emotions, domestic issues, feminine issues
Tuesday	Mars	Self-assertion, courage, more energy
Wednesday	Mercury	Communication, education and self-expression
Thursday	Jupiter	Money, prosperity, influencing people
Friday	Venus	Love, friendship, beauty, creativity and harmony
Saturday	Saturn	Overcoming obstacles, banishing negative energy, protection

Tip: According to the planetary days, the week is traditionally meant to start on a Sunday with the sun representing new beginnings and motivations. Saturday was traditionally the end of the week as Saturn is associated with endings. Yet nowadays we class Sunday as the week's end and it's no wonder we all feel miserable on a Monday because the moon is associated with emotions and feelings!

ASTROLOGY AND CRYSTALS

Certain crystals can complement your sun signs, so pairing stones that offer benefits that chime with your particular sign can make them extra powerful Magical tools. For example, a person with a sun sign of Pisces is naturally in tune with their emotions and sensitive side, so a calming crystal like aquamarine, which radiates calming vibes, is ideal. But these are only suggestions, and some crystals will resonate with you regardless of whether they are connected with your sun sign or not.

Aries: citrine, garnet, carnelian

Taurus: peridot, rose quartz, iron pyrite

Gemini: jade, blue lace agate, quartz

Cancer: moonstone, pearl, abalone shell

Leo: garnet, tiger's eye, carnelian

Virgo: red jasper, jade, kyanite

Libra: lepidolite, Iolite, chrysoprase

Scorpio: smoky quartz, black tourmaline, rainbow moonstone

Sagittarius: sodalite, seraphinite, Herkimer diamond

Capricorn: azurite, malachite, mematite

Aquarius: angelite, merlinite, lithium quartz

Pisces: flourite, aquamarine, amethyst

WORKING WITH THE MOON

Witches work in sync with the moon but we all feel its power and gain energy from its presence.

The moon has four main phases:

○ New moon: a time for new beginnings and setting intentions

☽ Waxing moon: a time for taking inspired action, transformation

● Full moon: a time for celebrating and giving gratitude

☾ Waning moon: a time for releasing and cleansing

It's a good idea to time different forms of Magic with the lunar phases. As the moon gets bigger (waxing), we work Magic for increase; as it wanes, we work Magic for decrease. So, when you want to bring something into your life, the ideal time for casting an affirmation or taking action is during a waxing moon. If you want to let go of something negative or unwanted in your life, working during the waning phase is key.

Check the phases of the moon each month with a calendar or diary (these often use symbols to illustrate the phases) and acknowledge this as part of your daily practice. You will find yourself more attuned to the subtle differences in lunar energy as the cycle develops.

'I don't believe in astrology,
I'm a Sagittarius and we're skeptical.'
ARTHUR C. CLARKE

Full moon power

When the moon is full, Magical energies are at their peak, which is why so many spells and rituals are cast under a full moon or when the moon is full.

There are several spells that work especially well and are suited to the unique energies of a full moon. These include:

 Money: Call upon the full moon's supercharging abilities and harness your Magical intent into money spells or expanding your wealth.

 Love: The full moon and romance go hand in hand. This stage in the moon cycle is ideal to open yourself up and become receptive to love. Try spells to bless an existing romance or ones to harness new love in your life.

 Banish unwanted conditions: The full moon is the moment the moon's energy begins to wane, which makes it a perfect time to rid your life of conditions you no longer desire – toxic relationships, stubborn health issues, etc.

 Empower your crystals: Set your crystals out on a white towel or sheet under the full moon, allowing them to absorb the moonlight to both cleanse and refresh their energetic potency.

 Clear and bless your home: Clearing your home and removing negative energies can be done at any time but during a full moon you'll benefit from extra Magical energies that will help you set positive intentions throughout your home.

 Personal goals: The full moon is a perfect time to empower your commitment and focus on achieving a goal – particularly when it comes to personal development.

 Career focus: Whether you want to start a new job, bring about a change in career or bless a job you are doing and enjoying, harnessing the expansive energies at work during a full moon is ideal.

Solve a dilemma: The very presence of the clear, bright full moon is seen as a way to help illuminate and bring clarity on issues you need to resolve. Use this energy to solve problems that might have been troubling you, or perhaps cast a spell to find a lost object.

Powerful Moon Affirmations

New moon: I see my intentions clearly and feel the pleasure of them as if they have happened.

Waxing crescent: I create a plan and take action to give it a chance to succeed.

First quarter: I move towards my goal with focus and courage.

Waxing gibbous: The universe and my power are now perfectly aligned.

Full moon: I am unstoppable. Now is the time to close in on my goal.

Waning gibbous: I have accomplished my goal and I celebrate my achievement.

Last quarter: I let go of the past and understand that my mistakes have taught me invaluable lessons.

Waning crescent: I rest in the knowledge that all is well and I reflect with thanks.

A Full Moon Power Spell

Banish unwanted conditions: On a piece of paper write down all the things you would like to release from your life, for example, addiction to something, jealousy or resentment.

Under the moon, read your list out loud and then set it alight in a fireproof container (this part is important unless you've mastered conjuring water as well).

Speak aloud to the moon: *'Now I learn the grace of letting go and the power of moving on. So mote it be.'* Repeat as many times as necessary. (The final phrase is a common way of ending a spell and can be translated as something close to 'So must it be.')

Moon water

Moon water is water that has been left out under the full moon so it is fully energized with the moon's power. Ideally it is rainwater that is then collected into a clean and sealed container ready for use.

It can be used in a number of different ways:

 In blessings

 To charge or cleanse crystals (see Chapter Four)

 To charge or cleanse other ritual tools

4

Cleansing Crystals
and Dispelling
Toxic Energy

'You know the world is a wondrous place when Mother Earth grows her own jewelry.'

Having been formed over millions of years by the action of water, wind and volcanic fire, the crystals we use today hold a life force and healing power from both the Earth and sky.

Crystals carry their own healing energies and act as transmitters and amplifiers of such powers. Each crystal has its own unique properties, but we can also empower crystals to hold prosperity, love or success energies that can be released when we need them in our daily lives.

WHAT CRYSTAL?

Ultimately, we are all crystal experts if we trust our intuition and allow each crystal to speak directly to our hearts. Their potent energies will expand our own innate healing powers to bring harmony to ourselves and others.

Crystals associated with healing include amethyst, rose quartz, clear quartz, citrine and black tourmaline. I will cover these, as well as a couple more of my favorite crystals, in more depth, as well as the significance of their different shapes. But the most important thing to remember is that crystals are personal and meaningful to only one person – you! So, go out and explore, research and get a feel for the hundreds of other crystals that Earth has so kindly gifted to us.

Let your inner self choose

I find it is important to be receptive to a crystal, and to allow yourself to be drawn to one that will have meaning for you. If you are in a shop, the simplest method is to stand in front of a group of crystals, relax, close your eyes, and when you open them choose the crystal you are most drawn to. If nothing strongly appeals, accept that the time is just not right and come back on another day when perhaps you will be immediately attracted to one.

There are certain crystals that are associated with different intentions, such as love, new beginnings, passion, spirituality, wealth and protection. And sometimes you might go out with the idea of buying a crystal that you have read can help dissipate a particular negative energy, but your unconscious leads you to look at another crystal.

Listen to that.

Follow that instruction.

Our subconscious might be picking the crystal that is right for us at the time. This is often the best approach to choosing crystals: quiet your mind and choose what you feel is right.

ROSE QUARTZ

Qualities: **love, peace, gentleness, confidence, balance, affection, tenderness***

I find this to be one of the most humble and yet most powerful of crystals. It turns us towards love, linking our hearts with that of the Earth and the universe.

Rose quartz is a healing crystal, used to help the recovery and restoration of people or animals. Wear it, hold it, travel with it, or have it by your bed at night. Meditate with rose quartz to bring love and compassion into your life.

* You will find that certain qualities, such as balance and intuition, are common to many crystals, as these often connect to fundamental energies shared by many natural sources.

Meditation Idea

If you're feeling down on yourself, hold a rose quartz crystal up to your heart and clear your mind. Sit with your emotions, both good and bad. Feel how powerful you are.

Concentrate on breathing, inhaling love and exhaling grudges or negativity.

Try to see the pink light of love that you are inhaling moving through your body, revitalizing your weary mind and surrounding your wounded heart.

Continue until you feel your essence has lightened.

Then repeat the affirmation: *'I open my heart to love, forgiveness and joy. I welcome all that is good in the world. I will cast the light of love.'*

Saying this will help in your quest to become a more loving person – both to others and yourself.

Pet protection

Associated with the element of water, rose quartz's healing properties are naturally fluid; they wash out toxic energies and emotions that have been trapped inside you.

Water which has previously had rose quartz soaking in it can be given to calm a hyperactive, scared or traumatized animal. It is ideal for animals who have come from a rescue home feeling agitated and distressed.

MOONSTONE

Qualities: **protection, hope, intuition, calm, relief**

Moonstone is one of the best crystals for absorbing the moon's energies, and when fully charged with lunar power it is used for healing.

Moonstone protects travelers, especially those that travel at night. If you are a shift worker and drive a lot during the night, keep a moonstone crystal in your car. Or if you are taking a long-haul overnight flight, perhaps find a moonstone charm to attach to your suitcase.

Tip: Put a piece of moonstone under the pillow of a child who suffers from night terrors. It will help balance out and calm wakeful children, allowing them to regulate their sleeping patterns.

CLEANSING YOUR CRYSTALS

Crystals absorb negative as well as positive energy and so will need to be cleansed at regular intervals. For example, amethyst can be used to help cleanse a room of negative energies (anger, resentment, jealousy) but it will retain an element of that negativity until it is cleansed. Cleanse any crystal that is new to you to remove the impressions of those who have handled it before. If a crystal feels dull or heavy, it is time to cleanse it and perhaps give it a rest for a day or so, especially if it is being used on a daily basis. Crystals such as selenite or tiger's eye that are kept in the workplace to protect against technological pollution will also require regular cleansing.

Ways to cleanse your crystals

△ Submerge them in salty water (ideally, take them down to the beach and dip them in seawater), then clean off the salt.

△ Bury them in the garden for a few days, letting the Earth cleanse and strengthen them.

▽ Leave them outside overnight in normal water to bask in moonlight – under a full moon is ideal.

▽ Hold in the smoke of an incense stick.

△ Burn sage and hold in the smoke.

△ Burn either a sage or cedar smudge stick (a tied-up bundle of the herbs) and hold your crystals in the smoke.

△ Use your breath to blow away the negativity with intention.

Wrap your crystal inside a dark silk cloth with a large unpolished piece of amethyst.

 Hold a crystal pendulum over your crystal (an amethyst or rose quartz pendulum is ideal) and pass the pendulum over the top nine times in a slow, counterclockwise circle. Then dip your pendulum into a bowl of cold water nine times and shake it dry. Finally, move the pendulum back over the crystals nine times in a clockwise circle to empower it.

CLEAR QUARTZ

Qualities: **clearing, clarifying, cleansing, balance, creativity, energy**

Clear quartz is probably the most versatile of crystals and can be used for any energizing, cleansing or healing work. It contains pure light and undiluted life force, which bring vitality, joy and health to those who keep it. I find it a great crystal to meditate with if I am in need of clarity as it improves my focus.

Keep a cluster of clear quartz on a meeting-room desk to encourage people to work together in harmony. They instill a sense of optimism and clear purpose in people who are generally more pessimistic or unwilling to accept new ideas.

Tip: Write down three positive things that have happened to you today. Read your list aloud while holding a smooth piece of clear quartz and give thanks. This positive ritual will help attract more positive things into your life so your list will get longer and longer!

ENERGY VAMPIRES

Do you sometimes feel deflated, low or running on empty after being around certain people? These can be friends, family, neighbors, work colleagues or strangers, and after spending time with them you feel hollowed out. That is because they are drawing out and feeding off your positive energy as they are unable to create or sustain their own life force in a positive way.

Types of energy vampires:

The guilt trippers

The jealous ones

The blamers

The fun removers

The gossipers

The whiners

The insecure ones

The short tempered

While it is important to acknowledge that people who display these traits often just require a kind word or appreciation, if energy vampires are constantly feeding off you and you can't manage or buffer the relationship, you will need crystals that help dispel negativity to create a shield around you. Crystals such as labradorite will act as armor against other people's draining energies, while black tourmaline also repels negativity that may be surrounding you. Wear either as a necklace or bracelet as your protection jewelery.

Tip: Fill a bowl with amber, amethyst, brown jasper and dark banded agate crystals in your home the next time you have a visit from an energy vampire. These crystals will also help calm a room where bickering seems to break out for no reason.

AMETHYST

Qualities: **growth, balance, healing, intuition, imagination, patience, acceptance**

Sometimes known as 'the beginner's crystal', amethyst is
a healing crystal that brings stability, peace and inner strength.
It is effective for both the mind and body. It is especially useful for emotional
healing, centering those who are overstressed and helping to calm those who
tend to be easily angered. It can also aid spiritual awareness, as well as prevent
overindulgence and intoxication.

BLACK TOURMALINE

Qualities: **protection, balance, stability, awareness, healing**

This crystal is often used in healing and protection spells.
If placed on your altar, it can help deflect and dispel negative
energy. It is therefore ideal for self-care rituals and spells, and for creating a shield
of protection. It can help focus our awareness in the present and works to dispel
drama – for people who struggle with their emotions, wearing a black tourmaline
pendant can help protect against the influence of external negative energy.

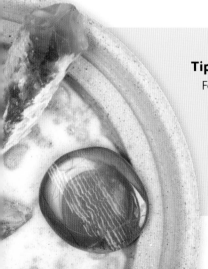

Tip: Hold a piece of black tourmaline in each hand.
Feel the crystals drawing out your anxiety, fears
and worry. They will absorb and dispel your
negative energy. Either in your mind or aloud,
say to yourself in a continual thirty-second
chant: 'I release negativity and I am protected
from negativity.'

'I've got a crystal for that.'

COMMUNICATING WITH YOUR CRYSTAL

It's important to understand that while you might use crystals for their own particular properties, you can also ask them for specific help with an area of your life. We're not telling the crystal what to do, merely harnessing its energy and making it effective for a particular purpose. This is sometimes referred to as programming your crystals with your intentions. Remember that you are using the innate energy of the crystal, not adding something that isn't there, so opt for a crystal such as a quartz which is multipurpose and could be programmed for any use – healing, protection, attracting love and so on.

Programming your crystal

Take your cleansed crystal somewhere quiet where you won't be easily distracted or disturbed. Hold the crystal up to your Third Eye Chakra, which is just above eye level, and say either out loud or in your head, 'I charge this crystal with my intention to [state your request].' When we empower crystals to hold our specific intentions we are also creating a special, unique bond between us and them.

GREEN FLUORITE

Qualities: **intuition, subtlety, softness, wisdom, stability, stimulation**

I find myself reaching for this crystal when I need to stimulate my memory, or I am learning something new and need to retain a lot of information. I call it my logical crystal. If I am feeling overwhelmed, frustrated or despondent, I will seek its calming and balancing energies.

Tip: If you are feeling unable to make a decision or are inundated with questions, go outside and find a peaceful spot. Hold a piece of green fluorite and repeat this affirmation: 'I am focused and in control, and I can make decisions with ease.'

CRYSTAL SHAPES

When choosing your carved crystal shape, it's best to keep in mind what you will be using your crystal for. For example, if it's for your altar, you might consider a standing point shape or pyramid. If you plan to carry it around with you, a tumble stone or heart shape is ideal (and sits snugly in the palm). You will also be intuitively drawn to a particular shape as your crystal needs manifest. Here is a list of the more common crystal shapes that might help clarify your thinking.

Tumble stone: A cut and polished crystal, one of the most common crystal shapes. They tend to be small but irregular and are versatile in that they can be carried around with you, placed directly on the body or scattered around the home.

Heart: Cut into a traditional heart shape, these crystals represent love, relationships and emotion. Small hearts can be carried with you to attract new love, while bigger ones placed around the home can help re-balance existing relationships or help heal emotional wounds.

Pyramid: These crystals have four triangular sides and a square base. They anchor and direct positive energies from the apex. They work well when placed around the home.

Crystal sphere: Crystal spheres are polished and perfectly round. They generate energy smoothly from all directions. They can slow down and neutralize harmful or negative energies. They need to be placed on a stand for display and to bring about a grounded energy to the home.

Standing crystal point: Sometimes called crystal towers, these are stones cut to a crystal point with a straight base that allows them to stand up. They help amplify our intentions through the apex and generate positive energy around the location where they are placed.

Wand: Solid crystals that have either a pointed or rounded end. They come in various sizes, but all have the same purpose: to direct the energies of the crystal into the chakras.

Cluster: A crystal cluster can be as big or small as the crystal points embedded in its base. If you want to cleanse other crystals or objects, leave them on top of the cluster overnight and allow them to absorb negative energy and recharge.

CITRINE

Qualities: **creativity, healing, concentration, vision, willpower, light, happiness, abundance**

This magnificent sunny yellow crystal is sometimes referred to as the 'sun stone' because it absorbs all the positive energy from the sun.

It is very much associated with setting and seeing through goals. It helps bring you the self-confidence to pursue what your heart desires. The positive energy of citrine helps to drive away darkness and fears. It is good for children, especially teenagers who might have problems at school, friendship worries and communication anxiety.

Tip: Try taking a piece of citrine with you the next time you go for a job interview or out shopping. It promotes and manifests success, stimulating wealth, prosperity and good fortune.

5

Embrace Your
Psychic Power
with Tarot

'Always trust your instincts, they are messages from your soul.'

When you open your first deck of Tarot cards you are becoming part of an ancient tradition that stretches back thousands of years. This powerful art form acts as a guide, a conversation with the universe, offering messages to you and only you, should you be open and aware of their meaning. The most effective way to read the Tarot is to use the cards to access your intuition and inner wisdom. The word intuition means learning from within. Most of us are not taught to use this sense but we all know that gut feeling when we have one.

The imagery on each card will connect you to this sixth sense – some like to see it as their subconscious mind. And from this place of inner power and wisdom you can discover how to make positive changes in the present and realize your future goals and desires.

SHUFFLING THROUGH TIME

Tarot cards, as they are known today, can be traced back to the mid-fifteenth century, when they were originally known as 'triumph' cards. These triumph cards had four suits – wands, coins, cups and swords – and contained numbered cards (one to ten) as well as court cards that included a queen, king, knight and page. The deck also included twenty-two symbolic cards that didn't belong to one particular suit and were used to play a game called 'triumph', which spread across Europe in the sixteenth century. It wasn't until around 1781 in both England and France that a deeper meaning was given to the cards. People believed that the pictures had a significant symbolic meaning, and they started using the Tarot cards for divination purposes.

HOW TO READ TAROT: THE BASICS

When reading Tarot for the first time it's important to focus on yourself and your own personal objectives. You need to have a set intention: a question you want answered, an idea you want to acknowledge, a thought you want to clarify. You are asking the cards for guidance, so you should keep that intention clear in your head as you shuffle the deck. Next, select any number of cards and either hold them in your hand or lay them on a surface. Your interpretation will come from within, sourced in your intuition.

The question you ask your cards, the number of cards you work with and how you interpret them are all personal. In this chapter, we'll work through some things to consider.

How to read Tarot cards intuitively

Take some time to get to know your cards before you go to them with a specific intention. This short exercise will help you develop your intuitive response when you later use the cards for a reading with a focused question.

1. Center yourself

2. Shuffle your cards with the intention of opening and focusing your intuition

3. Pull out one card and rest your eyes on it softly

4. What are your first impressions of the card?

5. Imagine the scene on the card coming to life. How would you describe what is happening?

6. Ask yourself: if the character started speaking, what would it say?

7. What three words best describe how the card makes you feel?

8. Try to practice this every day until you feel comfortable with what the cards are telling you and how they are making you intuitively feel

Uses for Tarot

 A focus for meditation

 A tool for clarifying goals

 A guide to self-knowledge and personal growth

 A tool for understanding the future

 A tool for helping us come into our own power

PICKING THE RIGHT DECK

Don't be afraid to seek out a new deck of cards if the one you have doesn't resonate with you, and don't be afraid to buy multiple sets until you feel drawn towards one in particular. Of course, if anyone gives anybody anything spiritual that is wonderful; the energy of giving should be praised. But don't shut out what you yourself are drawn to and have a connection with.

Buying a deck

There are some very rigid opinions about what deck you should buy and from where, but, like I always say, it's how you feel that is really important. Visit spiritual fairs, bookshops and mind/body/spirit workshops, or go online to search for websites and bookstores that have Tarot cards for sale. See what you are drawn to. The first deck of cards you buy or own doesn't need to define you. You are not beholden to one deck if it doesn't resonate with you.

Tip: Remember that Tarot cards won't give you a yes or no answer. The cards aren't good or evil. They have no power of their own, they are just cards. It is how you use their mystery and how you trust your instincts, your gut, your awareness that gives them power. They can be the mirror to your soul, the key to your inner wisdom and the storybook to your life. Be responsible with that power.

WHEN TO USE TAROT

Don't force the reading if the time isn't right. If you are having a hectic morning and there is a noisy intensity around, you aren't in the right state to open yourself to the cards. Take yourself away, try to embrace a quiet meditative state, and focus on the calm. You don't have to be alone when you read your cards but be mindful of distractions that might influence your understanding and interpretations. I will quite often do a reading first thing in the morning, when the energy of the day has a calm, fresh quality to it. Again, the timings and surroundings are all a personal preference. Be aware that your own state of mind will influence your reading, too. If you have just had an argument with someone or your mind is buzzing with things that need to get done that day, I would suggest waiting until your emotions are more stable and your to-do list is clearer. It's all about focus and allowing the cards to speak to you.

SPREADS

Don't worry too much about using a particular spread (the layout of the cards) when it comes to a reading. You'll find that there are spreads for the different times of the day, for the type of answers we seek, for occasions like birthdays and New Year's Eve – the list is endless! We all have our own favorite spreads. Maybe you prefer the more traditional ones, a one-card daily draw, or spreads you have created yourself.

One particularly simple spread, just three cards in a row, can be very revealing if related to the self and your personal happiness. Here are some ways to approach the cards, depending on the type of question or form of clarity that you are seeking:

(From left to right)

> *What is my dream? / What is stopping me*
> *(what is my fear)? / What is the reality?*
>
> *Who I was / Who I am / Who I will be*

What do I think is going on? / What is actually going on? /
What, if anything, can I do about it?

What should I embrace? / What should I erase? / What should I face?

What are my strengths? / What are my weaknesses? /
What do I do with them?

Tip: Always cleanse your cards after every reading. Your
energies will be left with each card you touch. Keep them
wrapped with cleansing crystals, or move them through
incense smoke after a reading. I always keep my cards wrapped
in a silk scarf. I place an amethyst crystal with the cards to
keep them energized, and I will regularly run the smoke
from burning sage through the cards before I use them.

'Tarot cards are our tools, they help us tune into our intuition. And they are such beautiful tools to work with!'

THE DECK

There are many different Tarot card designs, many different decks and no standard number of cards; however, most that you find today are based on the Rider-Waite system. This was a deck created in the early 1900s, and while the illustrations on the cards differ according to the various themes of the deck – nature, animals, dragons, fantasy – the meanings remain broadly consistent across all decks. Every element of each card holds significance. They contain color, characters, astrological signs, astrological elements – all of them different depending on the deck. This is why finding the right deck is a very personal process.

There are, however, some elements that most of them share.

The Major Arcana and the Minor Arcana

The Major Arcana (Arcana in this instance simply means group) represent some of life's big lessons, influences and themes. They include twenty-one numbered cards and one that is unnumbered, the Fool.

Tip: Shuffle your deck and think about a goal or a desire. When you feel ready, split the deck in your hands and hold the cards face up in each hand. The left-hand card represents what will hinder you and the right-hand side what will help you.

Below is a list of the Major Arcana and, very broadly, their themes:

The Fool —
new beginnings, spontaneity

The Magician —
action, willpower

The High Priestess —
secrets, intuition

The Empress —
motherhood, abundance

The Emperor —
ambition, assistance

The Hierophant —
marriage, tradition

The Lovers —
love, passion

The Chariot —
movement, determination

Strength —
care, responsibility

The Hermit —
loneliness, solitude

Wheel of Fortune —
destiny, fate

Justice —
court, commitments

The Hanged Man —
sacrifice, prophecy

Death —
rebirth, endings

Temperance —
home, balance

The Devil —
temptation, bonds

The Tower —
disruption, catastrophe

The Star —
hope, dreams

The Moon —
self-delusion, deception

The Sun —
achievement, success

Judgment —
transformation, calling

The World —
completion, travel

The Minor Arcana cards represent the more practical, daily ups and downs in life.

The Minor Arcana include four suits: wands, swords, cups and either circles or pentacles. Each suit in the Minor Arcana has a meaning related to a specific approach to life.

Wands: passion, creation, ambition

Swords: conflict, communication, intellect, aggression

Cups: love, relationships, emotions, intuition

Circles/pentacles: education, finance, health, business

The cards within these suits are numbered one to ten and also include the court cards: King, Queen, Knight and Page. The numbers on the cards can be broadly related to themes:

1. New beginnings, opportunity
2. Balance, partnership
3. Creativity, growth
4. Structure, stability
5. Change, conflict
6. Communication, cooperation
7. Reflection, knowledge
8. Mastery, action
9. Attainment, fulfillment
10. Completion, renewal

People study Tarot for years and still only touch the surface. When you're starting out, spend some time going through the booklet that comes with each deck, as it should fully explain the meaning and symbolism of each card. There are also traditional interpretations on how to read the cards, which are readily available online, but you can go with your gut instinct about the meaning. There is no right or wrong way, but be mindful of one thing: you are doing this for you, no one else. Go with the meanings that feel right for you.

> **Tip**: Seeing a Major Arcana card about a particular subject in one reading and then getting a Minor Arcana card about the same subject in the next reading could signify that this subject is becoming less important in your life.

Tarot and the Zodiac

Tarot readings and the zodiac complement one another, with each suit of the Major Arcana associated with specific signs of the zodiac – see the list below. Each offers more clarity and context to the insight offered by the other. So, a Tarot reading can help you better understand your daily horoscope and vice versa.

Aries – The Emperor

Taurus – The Hierophant

Gemini – The Lovers

Cancer – The Chariot

Leo – Strength

Virgo – The Hermit

Libra – Justice

Scorpio – Death

Sagittarius – Temperance

Capricorn – The Devil

Aquarius – The Star

Pisces – The Moon

ORACLE CARDS

Oracle cards are similar to Tarot in their purpose but not in their structure – I like to think of them as nonidentical twins. Oracle cards don't have Minor or Major Arcana suits, or court cards, like Tarot; they are simply a themed deck, with the cards often displaying written messages.

They can feature almost any kind of content – animals, angels, crystals, nature, fairies and so on. Because they mainly feature messages that give insight into the card you have picked, they don't require you to flex your intuitive muscles as much as Tarot cards.

For example, Angel Oracle cards are very popular. They have illustrations of angels and an uplifting phrase on each one. You can pick a card and read its meaning instantly. You will still have to untangle how the card relates to the question you asked but it gives you a quicker route to that answer.

In one case, I asked my Archangel Oracle cards if I should go to a business meeting that I was dreading. I shuffled the cards as I asked the question aloud, then cut the pack when I felt ready, revealing the Archangel Ariel card and her message: Be courageous and stand up for your beliefs.

I like working with Archangel Oracle cards. A deck was passed on to me by a relative and I was immediately drawn to them. Ultimately, whether you choose to work with Tarot or Oracle cards, your intuition will lead you to themes and imagery that you are emotionally connected to and can benefit from. It is as simple as saying to yourself, I enjoy looking at these cards, I feel a connection when holding them, and I want to develop a working relationship with them.

SHUFFLING YOUR DECK: THE JUMPER

While shuffling your deck in preparation for a reading, quite often — and this happens to us all — a card or three jumps out of the deck onto the table or floor. But what does it mean? Should you pay particular attention to that card and give extra significance to it? Or simply place it back in the deck and continue? Some people will put their jumper card aside and assign it extra weight. Others will simply put it back and carry on shuffling.

So, did the universe want you to pay particular attention to that card? Perhaps. But remember, some decks are made up of lots of cards and it can be tricky handling so many of them at once! You could spend a lot of time working out why you had five dropped cards on the floor that day, or you could put it down to a handling error. Simple as that. Whatever you decide, there is no right or wrong answer. It's down to your interpretation.

6

The Magic
of Nature

'Adopt the pace of nature: her secret is patience.'

RALPH WALDO EMERSON

Nature is all around us, whether we live in the countryside or in the heart of a city. Admittedly, it is easier to find when you live in the country but it is always there, and part of the ability to see nature even in a concrete jungle comes from being connected to it. Today, technology, work stress, family strains and the pace of life mean that people are becoming increasingly distanced and disconnected from nature. We are often unable to see the wonders she brings right to our very doorsteps.

Mother Earth's energy is one of the most powerful Magical tools at our disposal. We can see it in the flow of rivers, the movement of the breeze, and the strength locked into the trunks and branches of the trees. Connecting with nature heightens our awareness of our own energy and empowers it.

On a basic level, we know we like being outside. We feel great if we've had an afternoon in the sun or been blown around by the sea air, but we miss the connection with nature because we haven't engaged with it in an intentional way. Let's focus on forming that bond again.

BEING OUTSIDE

I feel my greatest connection to nature when I am by the sea, allowing the energies from the ocean and shore to pass through me, revitalizing me. When I hit the beach, I'm one of those who has to immediately strip off my shoes and socks, so I can feel the sand between my toes, and get that much closer to the flow of energy that connects us as living beings with everything that surrounds us. When you connect with nature in this way, visualize drawing this life energy into your own energy field. You can then direct it with clear intentions to help you heal, recenter and refocus.

There is nothing better than fresh air, sunshine and the sea to clear away the negative energy that has built up inside you – it can feel like an uncomfortable fullness. It needs to be released, and the best way to do it is to be outside, letting Mother Nature's energies flow through you.

Wind carriers

On a windy day, go and stand outside. Feel the air blowing wildly around you. Visualize the wind passing right through you, collecting all the negative energy and releasing it out into the open. Feel the power of the wind as it hits your cheeks, your limbs, the core of your body, and then focus on it lifting out all the negativity, carrying it away from you out into the universe.

Sun kisses

Face the sun and close your eyes. Feel the warmth on your face. Visualize the strength of the sun's heat breathing energy into every cell in your body, boosting and strengthening your energy and power. The kiss of the sun on such days is a symbol of true affection.

EARTH GROUNDING

Go outside and find a patch of land that is not covered by concrete or other man-made material. Stand barefoot, with feet flat on the ground, and close your eyes. Focus on your breathing and then say the following, either in your head or out loud:

'On this earth is where I stand,

digging roots deep into the land.

Fill me with your energy,

fill me with your strength.'

Feel your energy go down into the ground and bring back up the Earth's energy.

Connecting with nature through grounding is an ideal way to make a physical link with the Earth and re-energize yourself with the strength of Mother Nature. But it's not always possible to make an earthing link on a daily basis if you live in an urban environment. In these situations, there are simple affiliations we can make with nature in order to make a meaningful connection.

Earthing: The process of absorbing Earth's free-flowing electrons from its surface through the soles of one's feet. To ground is to pour your energies back into the Earth and feel the warm calm of nature entering your body in exchange.

Simple connections to nature

 Try touching five different plants or flowers on your way to work. Hold and feel the leaves between your fingertips.

 Shut your eyes and listen to the sounds around you, the birds chirping, the wind rustling through trees, grasshoppers or crickets in hedges.

 Look for spiderwebs on gates, fences or between tree branches. Take time to be thankful to that beautiful creation that nature has decided to share with you on that day, at that time.

 Look on the ground and in grass for insects, ladybugs, or worms. Accept that everyone and everything has their own unique place and importance in the world.

 Look for a tree near where you live and that you see on a regular basis. Look after it, clear away rubbish from it, talk to it and leave it gifts.

THE WISDOM OF TREES

If you can, right now, sit by a tree. Go and find one in your yard, garden, park, or woodland. Sit right under it with your back tight up against the bark. Close your eyes. Let the energy from the tree and Earth surround and embrace you. Soak up the energy and power with each intake of breath. Accept the wisdom of trees:

 They value their roots

 They embrace change with the dropping of their leaves

 They are still yet they are continuously growing

This is best done in solitude and silence. But forming a circle around the base of the tree with fellow witches allows the Magic of nature to penetrate those open and willing to make the connection.

Be grateful. Thank the tree for its strength, resilience and growth over the years. Either with your own words of thanks or the ones below, signify you are aware of the authority of this tree:

'Your roots are stretched in the earth,

growing stronger since your birth

and nothing will break them or you,

they endure,

I gain strength from your roots.'

> *Petrichor (noun) pe·tri·chor*
> *Definition: The smell of earth after rain falls*

'Nature doesn't hurry and yet everything is accomplished.'

LAO TZU

THE SEASONS

Seasons can present a challenge when connecting with nature. When the weather gets cold and wet, we don't want to go outside. We want to stay warm, safe and protected from the elements. But why are children happy to go out whatever the weather? They will discard their shoes and splash in the sea in the winter months; they will experience the purest enjoyment from running outside in the pouring rain. Animals are the same. Dogs live in the moment. They will become energized from the most cold, bitter, windy days, as if the power of the wind has run right through them and boosted their energies. They have made that connection.

Seasonal acceptance

Mother Nature has a purpose for all her seasons. It's important to connect and accept each seasonal change as it comes. No one season can flourish without the other – the spring will not feel so uplifting without the winter chill. It's important to engage with each season to allow the energies of the Earth and Magic of nature to inhabit your daily life.

SPRING

Nature springs into action with bright blooms bursting through the hard winter soil, casting their colorful quilts across the landscape. With its abundance of new energy, spring is an ideal season to cast our intentions of new beginnings and positivity with spring spells. It's also the season of the mother and time to give thanks to our Earth Mother. Ostara comes in the middle of March and is the second spring festival of the year, the egg symbolizing Ostara as we celebrate new life, new energy and new vigor.

'Came the spring with all its splendor, all its birds and all
its blossoms.'

HENRY WADSWORTH LONGFELLOW

Spring Ritual

Gather together any lists that you might have made in the past
year of big things that you wanted to achieve – New Year's
resolution lists are perfect. Light a yellow candle, and then say out
loud each of the following lines with clear intention and focus:

'Out with the old,
in with the new,
Ostara bring a changed view.
My dreams and plans are refreshed,
I will succeed with passion and zest.'

Now, look over your list again. Check off the ones you
have completed or that no longer apply and feel the
energy of spring flow into your plans for the future.

SUMMER

Summer is a time when we are reminded that the sun is an omnipresent power in the sky; we don't always see her when the other seasons have control, but she is there nonetheless. At the height of her power, we experience the longest day and shortest night – light signifying growth and expansion, dark signifying withdrawal and rest.

The sun has allowed Earth and nature to be in full bloom. Before the autumn harvest her intense heat energizes us. We become fiery, passionate and deeply sensual. There is a reason we use the term sun-kissed – we feel the love and energy from the sun as it heats and strengthens us. It's a time of empowerment and strong Magic.

Midsummer Manifestation Ritual

Make a list of everything you want to establish during the next six months. Be complete – include ideas related to life issues, relationships and career, as well as things related to personal growth such as confidence and clarity. At sunrise, with a vase of summer flowers next to you, light a candle and say aloud:

'I gather in the great power of this day, I honor the sun and her strength for I know I am in the season of her greatest power. I ask her to bring the last grace of her power in light to manifest my desires in the coming harvest.
I ask that this be [read aloud your list].
I affirm that I am able and willing to allow these wishes to manifest and I participate in the miracle of faith and creation.
So mote it be.'

AUTUMN

Autumn is sometimes referred to as the grand finale of nature, a lovely reminder of how beautiful she can be — the rich colors, the smells, the feel of the air and cooling wind around us.

It marks a period of change, recognizing the shift in Mother Earth as she refocuses, and acceptance of such transformation. Leaves do not cling to a tree, refusing to let go, just as we should accept that sometimes loosening our grip in one area of our lives will ultimately bring us greater strength and teach us resilience.

An Autumn Blessing

*'I welcome all the energy of autumn into my life.
I accept it is the time for transformation and reflection,
as the leaves fall away from their branches, my life
flows and changes peacefully.
With grace, I let go of anything that is not serving me
positively and I make way for many new blessings.'*

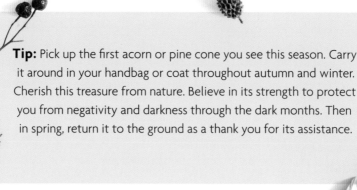

Tip: Pick up the first acorn or pine cone you see this season. Carry it around in your handbag or coat throughout autumn and winter. Cherish this treasure from nature. Believe in its strength to protect you from negativity and darkness through the dark months. Then in spring, return it to the ground as a thank you for its assistance.

WINTER

The sharpness of the first frost, the crispness of the air, thick white snow beautifying everything it touches — winter is a reminder that even when the dark and cold enter our lives, we can find beauty and wonder in the outdoors. Next time it snows, try watching a single snowflake fall to the ground. Acknowledge a kinship with that snowflake. No snowflake ever falls in the wrong place.

Snow Magic Rituals

Snow water: Gather snow in a cup and allow it to melt.
Use the snow water, which is simultaneously purifying and
energizing, to cleanse crystals and charge your Magic tools.

Snow cleansing for an object: Fill a bowl with fresh snow and bury
within it an object that signifies something in your life that you need
to remove. Say a blessing and then charge the bowl with this intent:
'As the snow melts away, so shall all negative energy melt away.'

Snow cleansing for you: Go outside and stand in
the snow as it falls from the sky. Let its cleansing
and calming energies invigorate and fill you.

Snowball release: Make a snowball and fill it with a
worry, bad habit or negative thought you want to get
rid of. Then throw the snowball as far as you can.

'I am grateful for winter. It reminds us that everyone and
everything needs some quiet time.'

KATRINA MAYER

A REMINDER FROM MOTHER NATURE

Have faith that you are where you need to be at any given time and that you will get to where you want to be eventually. Follow Mother Nature's example: the four seasons all have set intentions and each season accomplishes its objective. Enjoy the process of change, cherish it, absorb it and accept it. And never stop being grateful for her wonder.

7

Everyday Spellcraft

'And so, she decided to start living the life she'd imagined.'

Spells come in every size, shape and form. There are countless daily intentions, rituals, blessings and spell castings to be found online, as well as many others in books. Some are only passed on from witch to witch. If you do a little research, you'll be able to find the ones that work best for you, using the Magic tools you enjoy. Once you get the hang of casting spells, and a secure sense of how to connect with and wield the energy that surrounds you, you may even decide to create your own.

Remember, spells are all about focusing and harnessing *your* energy, and bringing it to work with the energy you are calling upon for a specific result. So be honest and exact in your intentions. Set yourself some positive, life-changing goals, and enjoy the results!

I have peppered the book with lots of spells and blessings as we have touched on various subjects. But the ones listed in this chapter cover subjects for which Magic is used the most: love, money*, career and protection/banishment. I have also sprinkled seven of my favorite daily positive affirmations in this chapter, too.

* Of course, money alone does not equal happiness (no witch believes that), but when times are tough, calling on Magical assistance is a way we can help ourselves.

Positive affirmation:
I have the power to create change.

Create an Intentions Jar

Find an empty jar and place it on a windowsill or somewhere you are likely to see it during the day. Whenever you have an intention you'd like to manifest, write it on a piece of paper and pop it in the jar. Don't forget to be specific. For example: 'I spend time exercising and feeling the benefits.' Or perhaps use it for a particular occasion. For example: 'I learn to play three songs on the piano,' or 'I win my game of pool next week.' Whenever you feel the urge, pick an intention from the jar and spend two or three minutes visualizing that intention. Then discard it and any that are no longer relevant – the jar is for a purpose, not just for show or to be forgotten.

BANISHMENT / PROTECTION SPELLS

Dispersing negative energy

You will need:

 A dark crystal, such as black tourmaline

 A source of running water (this is a great spell to do on a bridge over a stream or river)

Visualize a circle of light around you and hold the crystal in your hands. Place it over your solar plexus. Allow the negative energy and all those emotions associated with it – anger, resentment, jealousy – to flow into the stone. Raise the crystal to your heart and if it seems right, repeat: 'With this stone, negative energy be gone, let water cleanse it back where it belongs.'

Your negative energy and anger is now sealed inside the stone. Now drop or throw your stone into the running water.

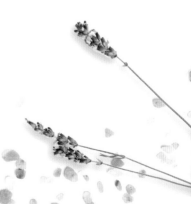

Bath of protection spell

You will need:

- Thirty minutes of undisturbed time to yourself

- A bathtub full of warm water

- Two cups of sea salt

- Two cups of white vinegar

- Incense to burn – sage is ideal

- Essential oils – rosemary or lavender

- Crystals – clear quartz or amethyst

Put all of the ingredients into your bath (except for the incense – put that on the side), then get into the water and relax. Focus on releasing negative energy from your body into the bathwater. Let go of negative thoughts and burdens from energy vampires you have connected with as the bathwater envelopes you. Then release the water while remaining lying in the bathtub. The water will carry away all the negativity, taking it down the drain, and out of your body and energy fields.

Positive affirmation:
I am grounded, I am loved, I am strong.

Three ways for empaths to protect and refresh their energy

Being an intuitive empath is a gift that allows you to sense, and absorb, the feelings and energy of other people and surroundings. However, it can easily become draining, so it is imperative that you are able to shield yourself and maintain spiritual boundaries – especially when in the company of negative energies.

1. **White light ritual**
   This shielding visualization can help protect you from an abundance of negative energy. Close your eyes and imagine a white light forming a protective bubble around you. You are now completely encased in this bubble. Repeat the affirmation: 'I only allow that which is for my highest good to enter.'

2. **Black obsidian ritual**
   Used by lots of empaths and witches as the ultimate shield against negativity, black obsidian can help calm the mind, and return a sense of peace and balance. Hold a stone in your hand and close your eyes. Breathe in and out in a slow, even rhythm. Repeat in your head or out loud the mantra: 'I am safe, my emotions make me powerful, and I am in charge of my emotions.' Keep repeating it for as long as you feel you need to. Afterwards, remember to cleanse your crystal of negativity.

3. **Raise your vibrations**
   Singing, dancing, having sex and laughing are all ways in which we raise our vibrations, and tune into happiness, hope and positive energy. While empaths can tune into the negative as well, shielding yourself by attracting positive energy by having fun will help limit the influence of the negativity. We attract what we are.

Positive affirmation:
I am taking steps to make my dreams a reality.

Burning and banishing spell

You will need:

 A small piece of paper

 A fireproof bowl

 A pen

Matches

Write down all the things you wish to banish on the piece of paper. This might be anything from the name of a person, specific worries or a personality trait that no longer serves any purpose for you (for example, procrastination or negative self-talk). Focus on what you have written, then set fire to the piece of paper and drop it into the bowl. As you watch it burn, imagine yourself without these things in your life. When the paper has completely burnt away, take the bowl of ashes out of your home right away, or as soon as possible. Scatter the ashes into the wind or simply dump them in your outside garbage can so they are far away from you.

Safety notice: Always be careful to keep the fire under control and dispose of the ashes safely once cooled.

A spell to bring a loving relationship to you

You will need:

 Wild rose petals

 A source of running water that eventually flows
into the sea, such as a stream or river

Close your eyes and visualize a person with the ideal qualities you want in a partner. Be specific and true to your heart. Then gather up the rose petals and take them to the water. As you scatter them in the water say aloud or in your head: 'As this rose moves out to sea, so true love will come to me.' Repeat the affirmation as you close your eyes again and visualize your ideal partner.

New moon, new love spell

You will need:

 A rose quartz crystal

 Pink rose petals

 A bowl of water

On the first night of a new moon, kiss the rose quartz and place it in the bowl of water with the rose petals. Leave it for seven days. At the end of the week, your crystal will be charged with powerful lunar energies. Carry it around with you to attract love into your life.

CAREER SPELLS

A spell for a new job

You will need:

 A candle (a tea light is good for this spell)

 A clear quartz point that has been cleansed with moon
water or sage smoke (clear quartz is ideal as it energizes
the body and keeps you focused on your goals)

 A piece of paper

 A pen

Place the candle either on your altar or on any flat surface and sit in front of it. Write at the top of your piece of paper, 'Thank you universe for my new job!' and then list below the qualities you visualize as important to you in your new job. For example, if proximity is important to you, write down: 'I work within fifteen minutes of my home.' If you want to earn more money, write down: 'I make X amount of money a month.' Or if having a good relationship with work colleagues is important to you, write: 'I work with people who appreciate me and my talents.' When you have finished your list, write your thanks and 'so mote it be' at the end. Light the candle and read aloud your list while holding the clear quartz in your right hand. Fold the paper into eight sections and then place it on the altar near the tea light. Place the crystal on top of the paper. Let the tea light candle burn down completely so it extinguishes itself. You don't have to watch it as it burns but be mindful of the flame if you leave the room.

Career change/promotion spell

You will need:

 A piece of paper

 A pen

A teaspoon of dried sage

 A green candle and candle holder

If you are looking for a new direction at work or change of career, cast this spell on a full or waxing moon. Write on the piece of paper the details of the change that you want to make – for example, the new job title you're aiming for. Lay the paper on a flat surface. Tear up the mint leaves and place them, along with the dried sage, on top of your writing. The sage will dispel negative energy and the mint will bring in positive energy. Light the green candle and put it in the candle holder. Then place the candle and holder on top of the paper. While doing this, visualize yourself in this new job, how it makes you feel, and what fulfillment it brings you.

After a few minutes or when you feel you have completed your visualization, take the candle and holder off the paper. Put it to one side. Allow the candle to continue to burn. Now take your paper with the herbs on top to a window or door that leads outside and blow the herbs from the paper into the air. Blow out the candle.

MONEY SPELLS

Summoning wealth spell

You will need:

 A green candle (the color green is associated with money, prosperity and the Earth)

 A green piece of paper

 Some matches

 A fireproof bowl

Light the candle (which could be placed on your altar) and make sure you are grounded in front of it as it burns. Visualize yourself receiving money and the feeling of receiving that money. Then write down your intention – for money, a pay raise, unexpected good fortune (windfall), etc.

Fold up the green paper as many times as you can. Before you light it, repeat in your head or out loud: 'This candle will bring wealth to me and I will receive money with all graciousness and thankfulness.'

Then carefully light your piece of paper in the candle flame before placing it in the fireproof bowl and watch it burn.

Positive affirmation:
Today is a wonderful day. Today I say goodbye to all that has brought me pain and I release it. I am free to go forward refreshed.

Money jar spell

You will need:

- An empty jar
- Seven coins (any will do)
- A bay leaf
- A piece of paper
- A pen

Write the amount of money you wish to receive on the piece of paper and drop it into the jar. Take the seven coins in your dominant hand and drop them into the jar one by one. As you drop each one, close your eyes and visualize them multiplying into many coins.

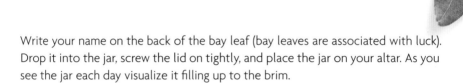

While dropping the coins into the jar, say out loud:

The money grows, the money flows

Coins that jingle, coins that shine

Come to me, your wealth is mine

Rewards I welcome

So mote it be.

Write your name on the back of the bay leaf (bay leaves are associated with luck). Drop it into the jar, screw the lid on tightly, and place the jar on your altar. As you see the jar each day visualize it filling up to the brim.

Once you have reached your money goal you need to remove the piece of paper and burn it, thanking the universe as you do.

Green aventurine crystal is also used for money spells as it is well known for attracting wealth and provoking random windfalls. Place one in your purse or wherever you keep money. Or you can use it to strengthen a money spell by holding it in your hand as you perform the ritual.

Casting a spell is simple and requires no great ingredients, fancy equipment, special platforms or wacky costumes. Casting a spell is simply identifying, raising and directing energy to actualize our intentions.

WHEN TO CAST A SPELL

You can cast a spell whenever you want; however, if you are going to take the trouble to collect the right ingredients, you might as well cast it at the most powerful time. Think about the time of day, the moon phases and the astrological calendar.

Timing your spells

Dawn rituals: Sunrise is an ideal time to perform rituals of purification and to bless new beginnings. Spells with a focus on work, study, travel and employment work best at this time of the day.

Midday: Make use of the sun at the height of its energy release by casting spells of strength, courage, opportunity and success.

Sunset: Cast spells for release, failure, pain and misery as the day draws to a close. Perform rituals for breaking addictions and negative habits.

Nighttime: Cast spells that will work to enhance your intuition and awareness, as well as spells and rituals that work on peace, releasing stress and nurturing love.

Positive affirmation:
I trust myself, I believe in me, and I have confidence in myself.

WHY SPELLS FAIL

Sometimes, even when you're doing everything right, a spell just doesn't succeed. It can happen to witches who have been casting spells for years, believe me. But why? There are lots of reasons for the odd spell failure, but if you are finding that you regularly struggle to get success, it might be something to do with one of the following:

1. **Types of spell**

   There are so many different ways to cast a spell, so many conflicting opinions and so many spells available that it's easy to find yourself pulled in different directions, trying to work with candles, an altar, lunar Magic, astrology, Tarot, crystals, herbs and more. While it's an appealing idea to master them all, in reality, you should really just go with the forms that suit you. Exploring the different styles is great (after all, that's how you find out what fits), but it is natural that you will be better at casting certain spells than others. Follow your strengths!

2. **Impossible Magic**

   Spells to win the lottery or influence political voting? Some spells may be just too hard for anyone. Of course, it is important to aim high and focus your spells on a specific intention with the belief that you are capable of effecting big change, but just as you might be working for one outcome, there might be lots of other witches working for the opposite outcome. Also, if something is impossible (and I'm talking something that is clearly out of whack with the natural energies that give witches their power), no amount of Magic is going to change that. You can't shoot fire from your fingers. You can't change yourself into a cat. Sorry.

3. **It is working, just not in the way you thought**

   This is quite common in love spells. You want your partner to be

more loving and attentive. So you cast the appropriate spell, hoping that your relationship will explode with passion and romance before your very eyes. But instead you and your partner start arguing. You eventually break up. That spell didn't work then. But it did! A short time later you meet someone who showers you with an abundance of love. So although the spell didn't work exactly the way you thought it would, it hasn't technically failed. Sometimes you have to have a little trust that Magic has its own way of showing you success.

4. **You worry too much**

Are you a natural worrier? Do you spend a lot of your time in an anxious state fretting about everyday things? Chances are you are bringing your heavy, worried state to your spells, which is effecting their chances of working. We all worry about the outcome of our spells ('Will it work?' 'What happens if ...'), but if you are constantly worrying about the outcome, it is likely that your excessive negative energies about the spell failing will outweigh all your spell intentions. Try to shift your mind into a more positive state during your spell and immediately after, or try distracting yourself with something that you enjoy. Put the belief back in your Magic.

Positive affirmation:
I am thankful for all that I have.

Let the Magic Begin

If you take anything from this book, I hope it is that the power of Magic lies within us all, and that when you find yourself in that place of power, of understanding, of acceptance, it will bring you peace and happiness. Generosity flows from those who have Magic running through their veins, so it's not just you that you'll be helping. What could be more powerful than that?

THE MAGIC WITHIN

We have explored the use of many Magical tools – from Tarot cards to crystals and astrology. But it's important to always keep in mind that these tools are just that – they are ways of connecting and harnessing the energies around us, and within us. We create our own spells and intentions. We find our own tools because our energy is individual and our Magic unique.

I Only Roll With Witches ...

I am in control of focusing my energies.

I have all the resources I need to find the
answers to any question I have.

I focus on self-awareness and experience peace, passion and joy.

I have unlimited capacity to grow, to learn, to
open myself up and to trust myself.

I learn from nature, my surroundings, the moon, the stars.

I am open to all the positive energies of people, crystals and cards.

I am a powerful, manifesting witch; I was born with Magic within me.

I hope you have found this book insightful and useful as you begin or continue your Magical journey. Remember, when you are working with the powers of the universe the possibilities are endless! Be thankful. Let go of anything that drains your energy. Acknowledge your own Magic and be prepared to see the change.

Love, Luna

Acknowledgements

To Lily, Henry and Tommy ... Always believe in yourselves and keep leaving your sparkle wherever you go.

Heartfelt thanks to Sarah Knight, Mel McAlpine, Susan Guru Gooderham and last but not least, Lesley Smith, the fountain of all Magical knowledge.

LB

About the Author

Luna Bailey has worked with crystal healers, Tarot readers, Reiki tutors and astrologers, as well as drawing on her own Magical experiences to produce this guide. She has published several nonfiction books, and has ghostwritten numerous autobiographies of strong women. She lives in Sussex with her husband, three children, two dogs and one cat – with the latter ruling the roost.

Index

A

affirmations 15–16
    balancing your chakra 31
    everyday positive 107, 108, 109, 116, 119, 121
    moon 59
    negative energy: a daily cleanse 33
    rose crystal – meditation idea 66
allergies 30
altars for Magic 36, 38–40
amethyst 68, 69, 71, 83
Angel Oracle cards 88
anxiety/worry 30, 121
Arcana, Major and Minor Tarot 52, 84–7
astrology 46–7
    crystals 56
    days of the week 54–6
    electional 48
    plotting your birth chart 52–4
    and Tarot 52, 87
    twelve houses 49–51
    working with the moon 57–61
    zodiac signs 48
autumn 101–2

B

balancing your chakras 30–1
basil 42
bath of protection spell 109
bay leaf 42, 118
bereavement 22
birth chart, plotting your 52–4
black obsidian ritual 110

black tourmaline 71, 108
blood pressure 29
breathing 29, 32

C

career/work life 16, 59, 68, 69, 114–15
cedar 68
chakra cleanse, mini 31
Chakras, seven 28–31, 34, 35, 72
chamomile 43
children 67, 75
chives 43
circulation 30
citrine 75
cleanse, mini chakra 31
cleanse, negativity energy 33
cleansing crystals 68–9
cleansing Tarot cards 83
clear quartz 69
clothes 32
color, altar cloth 36
color, clothes and 32
color Magic 39
colors and chakras 30
communication 29, 75
creativity 29, 38–9, 69, 75
Crown Chakra 28, 31
crying and healing 27
crystals 36, 56, 58, 64–75
    amethyst 71
    black tourmaline 71
    choosing 65, 74
    citrine 75
    cleansing 68–9